Modern

Swansea

Abertawe

Fodernaidd

An introduction to Swansea Modernism

Cyflwyniad i adeiladau Fodernaidd Abertawe

Words and pictures by / Lluniau a testun gan Catrin James
@swanseamodernist

Design and layout / Dylunio gan Lisa Brown
@lisa_in_leeds

Produced and published by / Cynhyrchwyd a chyhoeddwyd
gan the modernist © 2023

A prosperous Swansea town centre was erased to the ground in February's 1941 3 Nights' Blitz. The bombs were meant for the busy docks that curtailed Swansea Bay. A square mile of a grand Victorian town centre devastated. The medieval layout of the town gone.

Hard planning and on a budget, Swansea slowly rose from the ashes and work began on rebuilding the town centre in the early 1950s.

Building work was staggered and ongoing into the late 1960s, making the shopping centre a lesson in post war architecture design. Every retail block is different in its mid-century detail. The shop façades of 1951 have echoes of deco symmetry. This influence is the work of Ernest Morgan. He was Swansea's early 20th century County Architect and his mid-1940s plans reflect what we see today. Later in the decade a municipal look was favoured with a modernist outlook. It makes Swansea unique in the post war rebuilding across the nation at the time.

Fast forward 75 years to a city which is regenerating once more architecturally, but some of these post war buildings and details are beginning to disappear and they will be gone forever.

Come and visit, you'll enjoy.

Growing up in 1980s & 90s Swansea, Catrin found beauty in the post war municipal and civic buildings of the town. Shop front fonts, graphic-coloured tiles, repetitious railings, clean lines, forgotten door handles, concrete flowerpots, mid-century clocks and colourful Formica tables. These details were observed at a young age on the bus into town as she frequented the many cafes and milk bars with her mother for egg and chips on a Saturday.

Cafodd Abertawe ei chwalu i'r llawr dros y tair nosweth erllyll Mis Chwefror 1941. Roedd y bombiau i fod ar gyfer y dociau sy'n cyfyngu y bae. Naeth milltir sgwar o adeiladau mawreddog Fictorianaidd wedi'i dileu. Wrth cynllunio yn galed a heb lot fawr o arian, dechreuodd y gwaith o ail adeiladu canol y dref ddechrau yn y pumdegau.

Naeth yr adeiladu parhau hyd at ddiwedd y chwedegau gan wneud y ganolfan siopa yn wers mewn dilynio. Mae pob bloc yn wahanol gyda manylion canol y ganrif.

Mae ffasadau siopau y pumdegau cynnar yn adleisio manylion deco, a hyn oedd ddylanwad Ernest Morgan a oedd Bensaer Sir Abertawe ar y pryd.

Wrth ir degawd fynd ymlaen fe ffafriwyd gwedd ddinesig a modernaidd, sy'n gwneud Abertawe yn unigryw i unrhyw dref yn y cyfnod yma.

Dewch i weld am eich hyn, cewch groeso.

Naeth Catrin tyfu i fyny yn Abertawe'r 1980au a 90gau, a ddaeth i hyd i harddwch yr adeiladau dinesig y dref. Ffontiau y siopau, teils lliwgar graffig, rheiliau ailadroddus, llinellau clir, dolenni drysiau anghofiedig, potiau blodau concrit, clociau mawr a bwrddau Formica.

Gwelwyd y manylion yma i gyd ar y bws i'r dref wrth iddi fynd i'r caffis niferis gydai'i fam i gael bwyd ar Ddydd Sadwrn.

Abstract Sculptural Mural – Harry Everington 1969
Trinity Buildings, Central Clinic, Orchard Street, Town Centre

Harry Everington was the Head of Swansea Art College in the late 1960s. Harry and 2 students on the Sculpture course designed and created the large mural that resides on Central Clinic which opened in July 1969.

The mural is in 3 large sections. It is a mix of concrete and stone and has a lovely texture and creamy colour.

My Tadcu Irfon Morgan was the caretaker for the Clinic on its opening and he, my Mamgu and my mother lived in the caretakers flat on the top floor for 10 years. As part of my art practice, I have cleaned this mural a few times. Once for the Cultural Olympiad of Wales project 'Adain Avion' in 2012. Sometimes in small sections and once with a group of volunteers from the Swansea Bay Health Board Heritage Team.
The site is due for redevelopment in the next couple of years and the future of the mural is currently in discussion.

Murlun Cerfluniol Haniaethol – Harry Everington 1969
Adeilad Trinity, Clinig Canolog, Stryd Y Berllan. Canol y dref

Roedd Harry Everington yn Bennaeth Coleg Celf Abertawe yn y chwedegau a cynlluniwyd y cerflyn hwn gyda dwy myfyrwr.
Mae'r cerflun yn sefyll tu allan i'r adeilad. Agorwyd y clinig yn Orffennaf 1969.
Mae'r cerflun mewn 3 rhan ac mae'n gymysgedd o garreg a choncrit.

Fy Nhadcu oedd gofalwr y clinig pan agorywd yn 1969 ac roedd o, fy Mamgu a fy mam yn byw yn y fflat ar y llawr uchaf y clinig am ddeg blwyddyn.
Mae'r adeilad yn mynd i hailddatblygu dros y flynyddoedd nesaf a mae dyfodol y gerflun yn cael ei drafod ar hyn o bryd.

Archive image showing the clinic exterior

Swansea Civic Centre
J. Webb & C. Quick. 1982
The Beach, Oystermouth Road

Located on the curve of Swansea Bay, literally on the beach, the four storey Civic Centre is in typical Brutalist style. By the mid-1970s, the council needed a new location for its offices. It had Sir Percy Thomas's 1934 Guilldhall, but Swansea demanded a modern building and facilities.
The exterior features a continuous band of glazing with deep washed calcined flint panels.

Swansea Central Library and The West Glamorgan Archives Service both the busiest in Wales, are located inside with a café, all with exceptional views of the bay and Mumbles.
The interior architecture of the Civic Centre is on open levels of surrounding balconies with exposed concrete which is textured with a wood grain. Original tubular steel chandeliers and mature plants dominate the interior.

The concrete planters are integral to its interior design. The juxtaposition of the huge monstera plants next to the concrete moulded walls is exquisite. They soak up the white heat of the offices and give staff a sense of wellbeing.

I worked at West Glamorgan Archives Service 10 years ago. Working in the building felt luxurious and super modern, tactile and glamorous. What other civic buildings ask you to shake your feet of sand before you enter?

The entrance signs are displaying the free services available to the people of Swansea. Get housing advice, research Swansea's post war redevelopment, rent Polanski's Cul de Sac, take a book out on Welsh socialism and have a cup of tea. The Civic Centre has it all.

These services are moving to the city centre in the next few years.

Swansea Council have teamed with Urban Splash to redevelop the site as its location is gold.

Canolfan Dinesig Abertawe
J. Webb & C. Quick. 1982
Y Traeth, Heol Ystumllwynarth

Wedi'i leoli ar y traeth, mae gan yr adeilad 4 llawr mewn arddull frutalaidd nodweddiadol.
Roedd angen lleoliad newydd ar swyddfeydd y cyngor. Roedd ganddyn Neuadd y Ddinas 1934, Percy Thomas ond roedd angen cyfleusterau modern i'r ddinas newydd.
Mae'r llyfrgell canolog ac Archifau Gorllewin Morgannwg yn yr adeilad gyda golygfeydd eithriadol o'r bae.
Mae'r adeilad tu fewn ar lefelau agored gyda choncrit amrwd.

Mae'r arwyddion mynediad yn dangos y gwasanaethau sy'n rhad ac yn ddim i bobl Abertawe. Mynnwch gyngor ar dai, ynchwiliwch hanes y ddinas yn yr Archif, llogwch ffilm Ewropeiadd a darllenwch am sosialaeth Cymraeg a cael paned. Mae gan yr adeilad popeth.

Mae Cyngor Abertawe yn mynd i weithio gyda Urban Splash i rhoi dyfodol newydd iddo.

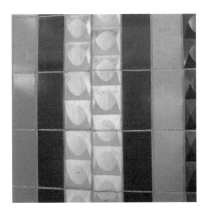

Swansea Market

Swansea's Victorian red bricked market was destroyed in the 3 Nights' Blitz of February 1941. Designed by Sir Percy Thomas & Son and built by Robert M Douglas Limited, the 'new' Swansea Market opened 20 years later.

Made of steel arched portal frames and glass, the roof spans 192 feet and floods the building with natural light. Swansea Market is a marvellous example of British post-war architecture which was paralleled in the other heavily bombed towns of Britain. Floor finishes are a combination of granolithic paving and ceramic tiles, all set in an aesthetically pleasing pattern. The few walled areas are covered with blue, white and grey tactile tiles, and are still intact today as is our wonderful mid-century clock that tells the time for shoppers to get their bus home on time.

Combining space and function, the Market seamlessly connects with the surrounding redevelopment of Swansea's town centre.

GOWER BUTCHER

EST. 1878

Shop

PORC
.WALES

LOCAL WELSH
EGGS

EVAN REES
SALTED
BUTTER

EVAN REES
TUB
ATTER
STE THE

SALTED
WELSH

C
1-30

C
£2-05

3011 23

Welsh Produce

Marchnad Abertawe

Dinistriwyd Farchnad Fictorianaidd Abertawe yn yr ail rhyfel byd yn mis Chwefror 1941.
Wedi'i dylinio gan Percy Thomas a'i Fab a'i hadeiladu gan Robert M Douglas Ltd, agorwyd y farchnad 'newydd' ym 1961.

Wedi'i gwneud o fframiau dur a gwydr, mae'r to yn ymestyn dros 192 troedfedd ac yn gorlifio'r adeilad gyda golau naturiol.

Mae'r farchnad yn enghraifft arbennig o bensaernïaeth Brydeinig ôl ail rhyfel byd

Mae gan y farchnad manylion esthetig prydferth fel wal teils ceramig, llawr gyda patrymau o feinil ac wrth gwrs y gloc enfawr canol y ganrif sy'n dweud yr amser cywir i helpu siopwyr.

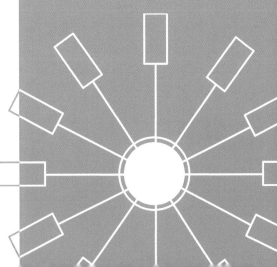

The Kardomah Café

The Kardomah Café opened its doors on its new Portland Street premises within Morris Buildings in 1957. Its previous location was on Castle Street and that's where Dylan Thomas and his 'Kardomah Gang' met and discussed the culture of the day. Castle Street was bombed in the 3 Nights' Blitz.

The interior of The Kardomah is untouched to its opening of 1957 and it is a joy to behold. Coffee paraphernalia adorn the walls and Bialetti pots of all shapes and sizes and traditional coffee tins are high up on the shelves.

The patterned Formica tables, the graphic tiled wall, the chairs, mosaic wall and pillar, the wooden panelled back wall with copper art reliefs and the sputnik style coat hangers all original.

The Luporini family have run The Kardomah since 1970 and their service is second to none and everyone gets a welcome.

Every time you walk through the doors, the smell of coffee beans, which you can buy freshly ground take you to a special time and place, which is that moment.

I'm there every week having lunch. There's nowhere else I want to be.

Agorwyd drysau Caffi Kardomah ar Stryd Portland ym 1957. Roedd y caffi wreiddiol ar Stryd y Gastell a dyma lle aeth Dylan Thomas a'i Kardomah Gang i ddrafod diwylliant y dydd. Cafodd Stryd y Gastell ei fomio yn y 3 Nights' Blitz.

Mae dodrefn Y Kardomah i gyd yn wreiddiol i'w agoriad a mae popeth yn edrych yn anhygoel heddiw fel petai yn newydd spon. Bwrddau Formica, wal efo teils graffig lliwgar a cadeiriau moethus. Y teulu Luporini sydd wedi rhedeg Y Kardomah ers 1970 a mae croeso arbennig i bob un sy'n dod trwy'r drysau. Mae arogl cryf coffi ffres yn eich cyfarch pob tro a phob math o goffi ar werth tu nol y gownter.
Does dim lle yn y byd well na'r Kardomah byth?

Regeneration is happening all over Swansea and many post war details are being lost in the process.
I could see that a small early 1960s precinct on the way out of the city centre was beginning to have attention by a local housing organisation. Barriers were being put up and one of the shops was having a refit. Swansea's last remaining concrete bin sat outside the Chinese take away in said precinct. There used to be roughly 7 of these dotted around the town centre since the early 1960s but they'd all disappeared as the 21st century kicked in.

In summer 2021 I got in touch with the housing organisation Coastal and enquired on the future of the concrete bin. It looked like its days were numbered.

I immediately spoke to the builders involved and they and Coastal were happy to take it out of the ground for me and were really positive and understood why I wanted to save it (it has a long iron base that fed into the ground below, like post boxes have) and having contacts at Swansea Museum, the future of the concrete bin was solid.

After 60 years of serving the Dyfatty area of town, the concrete bin is now part of Swansea Museum's post war collection.
The concrete bin is now part of the bigger story of the post war regeneration of Swansea.

It shows us how easy it is to erase the banal objects of our everyday life, the incidental bystanders in our social history. In 60 years, this rare object will give an insight of post war public furniture design, materials used at the time and how it feeds into the redevelopment history of post war Swansea.

Bin on Princess Way, c.1973

Bin outside Price's Newsagents, Kingsway, c.1973

112   1
114   1
116   1

Dyfatty shop precinct from behind
and above taken by Irfon Morgan c.1964

Mae adfywiad yn digwydd ar draws Abertawe i gyd ac mae llawer fawr o nodweddion diluniol y chwedegau yn mynd ar goll yn aml iawn y dyddiau yma.

Roeddwn gallu gweld bod ardal siopa yn yr ardal Dyfatty yn cael sylw gan sefydliad tai lleol. Roedd bin concrit olaf Abertawe yn sefyll tu allan y tecawe yn y ganolfan yma. Roedd arfer fod tua 7 o rhain o amgylch Abertawe, ond ers dechrau'r ganrif, hwn oedd yr unig un oedd yn sefyll.

Yn Haf 2021 nes i siarad a'r sefydliad tai lleol Coastal, a gofynnais am beth oedd dyfodol y bin concrit yma. Dim dyfoldol i fod yn honest. Arol siarad gyda Coastal a'r adeiladwyr, naethom nhw tynnu y bin allan or pafin i mi a nawr mae'r bin yn nghasgliad Amgueddfa Abertawe. Arol gwasanaethu yr ardal Dyfatty am 60 mlynedd, mae'r bin efo dyfodol concrit!

Mae'r bin yn rhan o stori ailddatblygiad Abertawe ar ol ail rhyfel byd a hefyd rhan o hanes cymdeithasol ein dref ni, sy'n bwysig i ddehongli hanes ein dyfodol.

Kingsway / Ffordd Y Brenin

The Kingsway opened in November 1950 on what was previously an old road called Gower St.
It is a long thin strip of 3 storey retail buildings with Munipcal façade detailing. The Kingsway has housed cafes, pubs, clothes shops, a famous hairdresser, a hotel, restaurants and more famously nightclubs.

The Kingsway was the centre of Swansea's night life for decades with clubs and pubs called The Top Rank, Barons, The Hanbury, Martha's, Harpers, Ritzy, Oceana, The Valbonne, Central Park, Time, Envy, Monroe's, Quids Inn, Rumours, Sin City, The Pool Sanctuary, Escape, Jumpin' Jacks and many others.

Agorwyd Ffordd Y Brenin ym mis Tachwedd 1950.
Mae'n ffordd hyr o adeiladau fodernaidd efo manylion gwahanol ar bob
ochr allanol.
Dros y blynyddoedd mae siopau dillad, caffis, tafarnau, gwestai ac enwedig
y clwbiau nos, lle ddaeth busiau llond dop o bobl yn dod o filltiroedd, pob
wythnos am ddegawdau.

Many buildings were subsequently built with stone cladding especially those around The Kingsway College Street roundabout and the west side of High Street. It looked modern and with nice little minimal nods to deco and classicism.

Adeiladwyd llawer o adeiladau wedi hynny gyda chladin carreg yn enwedig yr rhai Gogledd Ffordd Y Brenin tuag at Y Stryd Fawr.
Roedd yn edrych yn fodern a gyda nodau bach neis i deco a chlasuriaeth.

Former 'Wildings' Department Store

The Kingsway today is still a busy thoroughfare but not so much a shopping area. It's had its issues due to so many changes to its traffic layout over the last few decades. Bring back the roundabouts, they were great.

Heddiw mae Ffordd Y Brenin yn brysur fel arfer. Mae'r cynllun wedi newid dros yn flynyddoed. Beth oedd yn anghywir am y cylchfannau?

Former Swansea Savings Bank

Swansea's gem of a music venue The Bunkhouse is located on a strip of post war builds that have seen a change over the decades. The neo Georgian façade is typical of the range of styles that dominate The Kingsway however each build has continuity with their 3 floors. Always a social place to enjoy, the building was originally The Swan pub and then O'Neills Irish Bar in the 1990s.

Mae'r Bunkhouse yn lle arbennig i weld cerddoriaeth byw. Mae gan yr adeilad tair llawr a mae'n mewn steil 'neo Georgian' a oedd yn boblogaeth yn y cyfnod yma.

Former TSB Bank at Kingsway

Shaws the Drapers at 41 Kingsway

The Kingsway has junctions at each end where roundabouts once stood to shift the motor car around Swansea's main shopping area.
It is reminiscent of Ernest Morgan's (Swansea's early 20th century County Architect) 'Boulevard' plans of the mid 1940s that were all about creating a streamlined modernist, clean and efficient town plan.

Mae gan Ffordd Y Brenin cyffyrdd ar bob pen. Mae'n atgof i gynllun Ernest Morgan, prif Bensaer Abertawe ar y pryd. Fe oedd eisiau rhodfa fodern a symlach fel sydd gennym ni heddiw.

Portland House / Tŷ Portland

The first permanent building using steel construction and concrete was Portland House on the corner of Portland Street and The Kingsway. It was originally the C&A store then Mothercare and now a YMCA charity shop and now has student accommodation above its floors.

Yr adeilad parhaol cyntaf yn defnyddio adeiladu dur a choncrit oedd Tŷ Portland.
C&A oedd y siop cyntaf yna wedyn Mothercare am blynyddoedd. Siop elusen YMCA sydd yna nawr yn gwerthu dodrefn ac mae llety myfyrwyr ar y lloriau uwchben.

Morris Buildings

Morris Buildings is iconic for its marvellous clock and 1956 date on display. It proudly gives us a time when Swansea was in its mid-century glory. Morris Buildings sits smart on the corner of The Kingsway and Portland Streets.

Mae pawb yn gyfarwydd efo Morris Buildings a'i cloc eiconig sy'n taro'r amser i pan oedd Abertawe yn ysblander canol y ganrif.

Mayflower Restaurant / Co-op Bank

The Mayflower Restaurant was completed in 1953 and had a restaurant on both its floors. Today it still looks smart which makes the original detailing stand out. It was until recently a Co-op Bank.

Agorwyd yr adeilad ym 1953 fel bwyty The Mayflower. Heddiw mae'n adeilad smart, a dim ond yn ddiweddar roedd yn Banc y Co-op.

Boots The Chemists / McDonald's

Work started on the substantial 4 storey Boots the Chemists on Princess Way in 1952. The building is in good condition 70 years later. It dominates the area looking onto Castle Square with its repetitious square windows, red brick and dotted shelter overhang. A perfect example of a post war retail build. It has been McDonald's since the late 1980s. Let's hope it stands proud for another 70 years.

Dechreuodd gwaith adeiladu siop wreiddiol Boots The Chemist ar Ffordd Tywysoges ym 1952. Mae'n adeilad godidog ac mewn cyflwr da heddiw arol 70 mlynedd. Mae'n adeilad berffaith sy'n dangos llawer o maylion y cyfnod.

Boots The Chemists paper bag, 1966
With thanks to Dan Thompson for sharing

Religious Spaces / Llefydd Crefydd

Saint Benedict's Catholic Church, Sketty
Thomas Price ARIBA of F.R. Bates, Son & Price, 1961

Taking cues from Le Corbusier's famous chapel at Ronchamp, Saint Benedict's Catholic Church is a modernist joy to behold with its repetitious square and angular windows, curved ambulatory and imposing bell tower.

Mae nodweddion o gapel Ronchamp gan Le Corbusier ar yr eglwys yma.
Mae'n adeilad modernaidd arbennig iawn gyda'i ffenestri onglog ailadroddus.

Blessed Sacriment Catholic Church,
Gorseinon, 1967
Robert Robinson in partnership with
John Petts
Stained glass by John Petts and
Paul Quail

The church is circular and from
above gives an impression of a
modernist circus tent.
The wonderful cross stained-glass
windows punctuate all around the
church.
It has been listed by CADW for its
innovative church design which
takes from Liturgical principals. As
the church is elevated, you can
see the red sculptural cross on its
roof from miles around.

Mae'r egwlys yn grwn ei
ddynodiad efo to sy'n debyg i
babell syrcas.
Mae yna ffenestri lliw wedi'i
mewnosod yn y siapau croes o
amgylch yr adeilad.
Mae CADW wedi'i rhestri a
gallwch gweld y groes ar ben y
to am filltiroedd.

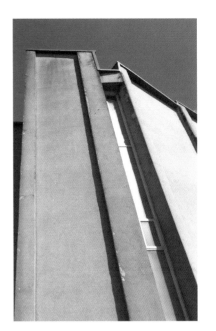

Singleton Park Hospital Chapel, 1978
Architect unknown / Pensaer di-enw
Windows designed by Celtic Studios / Ffenestri lliw gan Celtic Studios

This angular chapel is located at Singleton Hospital.
Built as a chapel it offered chaplaincy and spiritual care for staff and visitors.

Mae'r capel wedi'i osodi ymhlith Ysbyty Singleton. Naeth y capel cynnig
caplaniaeth a gofal ysbrydydol i ymwelwyr yr Ysbyty.

Singleton Hospital Side Entrance Hall / Neuadd a Derbynfa Ysbyty Singleton

This inviting hallway leads you into the Radiology Department of Singleton Hospital, which is located a stones' throw from the beach. The hallway is tall and large with municipal and neo Georgian detailing. It opened in 1958 and it was designed by Architect D. Garbutt Walton.

Mae'r neuadd yma yn eich arwain i adran Radioleg Ysbyty Singleton.
Mae'r ysbyty dros yr heol i Fae Abertawe ar traeth.
Agorwyd yr ochr yma or ysbyty ym 1958. Dilynwyd gan y bensaer D. Garbutt Walton.

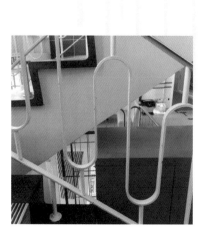

Gone But Not Forgotten /
Wedi Mynd Ond Heb Anghofio

Abstract sculptural door handle
Handlen drws cerfluniol haniaethol
Siop Elusen British Red Cross
Charity Shop
High Street/Y Stryd Fawr
Lost/Wedi'i golli 2017

Knitters & Sewers World

A haberdashery like no other.
A portal to all the fabrics and
making you feel like you were in
1971 at all times.

Sorely missed.

Siop ffabrig gorau erioed. Fel
mynd nol mewn amser.

Lost/Wedi'i golli 2020

Odeon/Top Rank/Tesco/Ritzy etc.
Kingsway/Ffordd Y Brenin
Lost/Wedi'i golli 2018

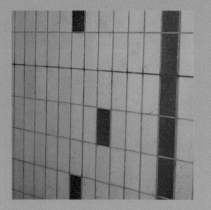

1966

Teils a tanfordd 1966 underpass & tiles
Connected Prospect Place and Wind
Street
Lost/Wedi'i golli 2012

David Evans Department Store
Ffordd Tywysoges/Princess Way
Lost/Wedi'i golli 2005

Welcombe House, The Strand/Y Strand
Lost/Wedi'i golli 2020

Covelli's Fish and Chip Restaurant
Heol Newton Road
Lost/Wedi'i golli 2005
Sign is now in Swansea Museum's collection
Arwydd yng nghasgliad Amgueddfa Abertawe

Albert's Caff
High Street/Y Stryd Fawr
Gorseinon
Lost/Wedi'i golli 2020

OUT IN

Espresso Bar Café
High Street/Y Stryd Fawr
Lost/Wedi'i golli 2019

The Windsor Café Fish and Chip Restaurant
Stryd Craddock Street
Lost/Wedi'i golli 2016

Original 1961 ceramic tiles on North Hill
flats/Teils wreiddiol
Jones Terrace/Evans Terrace/Wilks Row
Lost/Wedi'i golli 2022

Original 1957 tiles uncovered
from underneath shop sign/
Teils wreiddiol wedi'i
ddadguddio
Kingsway/Ffordd Y Brenin
Lost/Wedi'i golli 2014